Jim Brown

GREATEST RUNNING BACKS

LaDainian Tomlinson

NFL HALL OF FAMERS

GREATEST RUNNING BACKS

JOE TISCHLER

CREATIVE SPORTS

Franco Harris

CREATIVE EDUCATION / CREATIVE PAPERBACKS

Published by Creative Education and Creative Paperbacks
P.O. Box 227, Mankato, Minnesota 56002
Creative Education and Creative Paperbacks
are imprints of The Creative Company
www.thecreativecompany.us

Design and production by Blue Design (www.bluedes.com)
Art direction by Rita Marshall

Images by Getty Images/Al Messerschmidt, 28, Andrew D. Bernstein, 22, Bettmann, 4–5, 10, 11, 12, 32, Bill Eppridge/Time Life Pictures, 7, Bob Gomel/Time Life Pictures, 1, Brad Mangin, 29, Focus On Sport , cover, 3, 6, 7, 9, 15, 17, 21, 26, George Tiedemann, 18, Gregory Shamus, 7, Kidwiler Collection, 7, Kirby Lee, 2, Michael Smith, 25, Michael Zagaris, 6, 19, NFL/Pro Football Hall of Fame, 6, Rick Stewart, 30, TIMOTHY A. CLARY, 6; Wikimedia Commons/Don Cormier, Los Angeles Times, 14, Gonzo fan2007, cover (background)

Library of Congress Cataloging-in-Publication Data
Names: Tischler, Joe, author.
Title: Greatest running backs / Joe Tischler.
Description: Mankato, Minnesota : Creative Education and Creative Paperbacks, [2026] | Series: Creative sports: NFL hall of famers | Includes index. | Audience: Ages 8–12 | Audience: Grades 4–6 | Summary: "Photo-driven and stat-filled, this middle-grade NFL title showcases 11 of pro football's greatest running backs enshrined in the Hall of Fame, from Steve Van Buren and Walter Payton to Emmitt Smith and LaDainian Tomlinson"—Provided by publisher.
Identifiers: LCCN 2024048109 (print) | LCCN 2024048110 (ebook) | ISBN 9798889896173 (library binding) | ISBN 9781682777831 (paperback) | ISBN 9798889896975 (ebook)
Subjects: LCSH: Running backs (Football)—United States—Biography—Juvenile literature. | Football—United States—Juvenile literature. | National Football League—Juvenile literature.
Classification: LCC GV939.A1 T58 2026 (print) | LCC GV939.A1 (ebook) | DDC 796.332092/2 [B]—dc23/eng/20231120
LC record available at https://lccn.loc.gov/2024048109
LC ebook record available at https://lccn.loc.gov/2024048110

Printed in India

Walter Payton

60

MOSS
81

TAYLOR
56

42
42

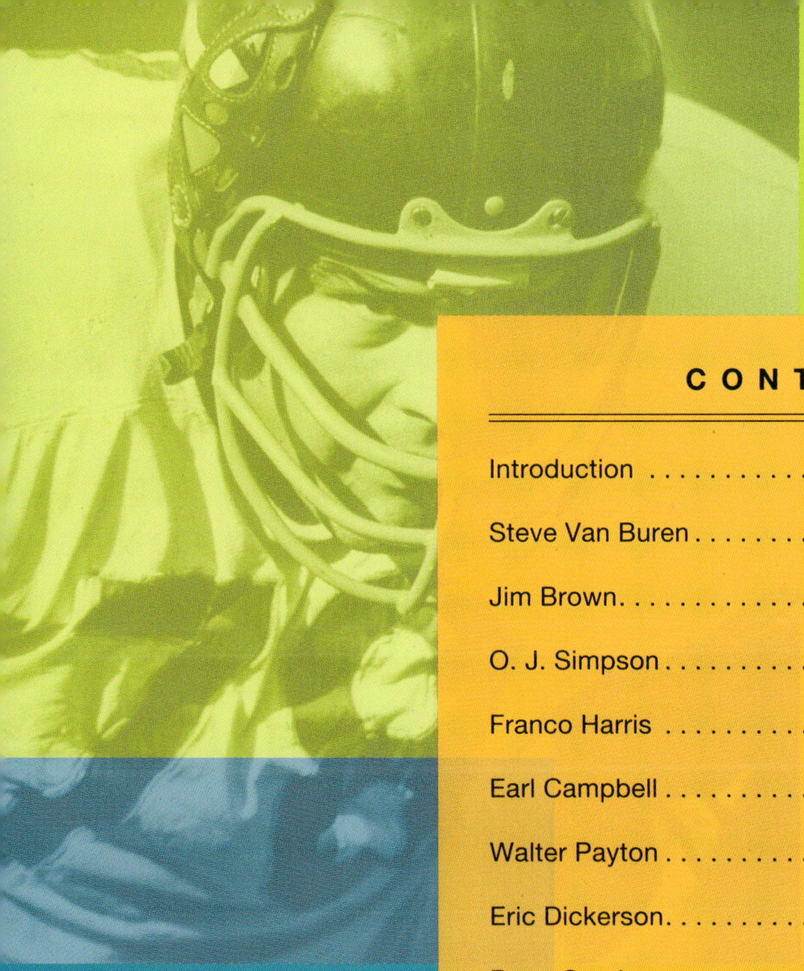
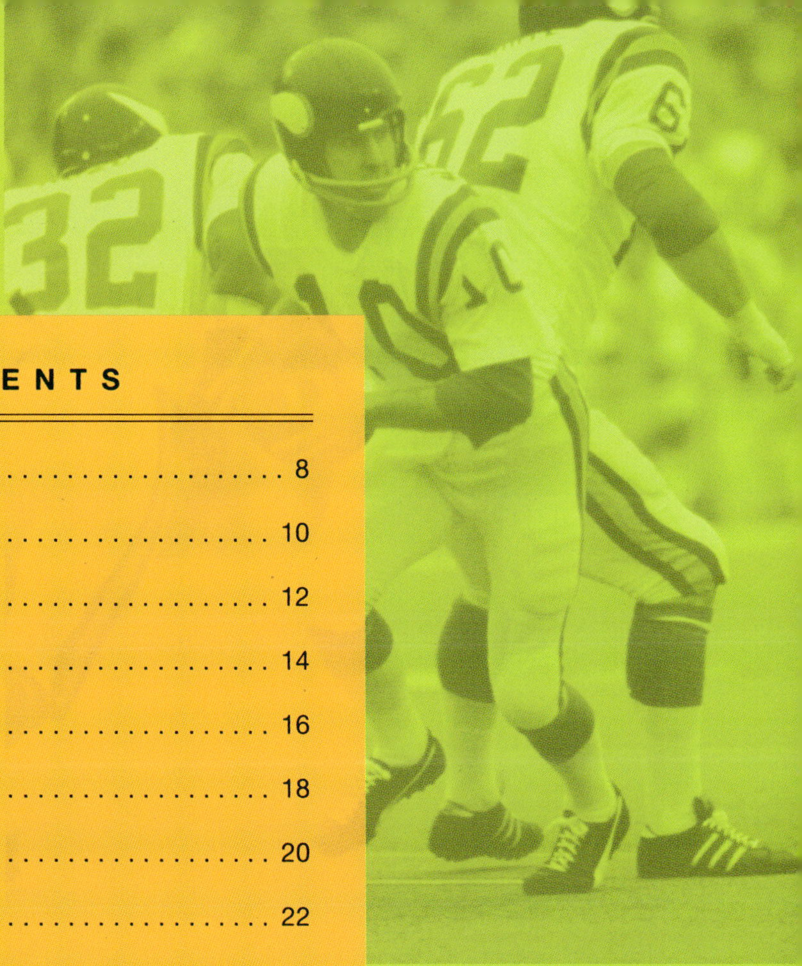

CONTENTS

TIMEOUT

INTRODUCTION

It's the fourth quarter of a playoff game between the Detroit Lions and the Dallas Cowboys. A trip to the National Football Conference Championship Game is at stake. The Lions lead. A touchdown will put the game out of reach. Detroit running back Barry Sanders takes the ball on the Cowboys' 47-yard line. He explodes. He's knocked at the 43 but keeps going. He slips past at least six more defenders before hitting the end zone. Touchdown!

Running backs are some of the most versatile players on offense. They are also called halfbacks and fullbacks. They combine power and speed with quick decision-making skills. All running backs who play for the National Football League (NFL) are at the top of their game. But only a handful can be called Hall of Famers.

The Pro Football Hall of Fame honors 378 past players, coaches, and sport contributors. Of those, about 40 are running backs. This book highlights 11 Hall of Fame running backs whose careers reached above and beyond. This list isn't a ranking. Players are ordered by the year they were enshrined.

Barry Sanders

STEVE VAN BUREN (1920–2012)
HALFBACK
PHILADELPHIA EAGLES SEASONS: 1944–51
HALL OF FAME CLASS: 1965
AWARDS/HONORS: MEMBER OF NFL 75TH/100TH ANNIVERSARY TEAMS, 7X ALL-PRO (5X FIRST TEAM), 1940S NFL ALL-DECADE TEAM, 2X NFL CHAMPION

STEVE VAN BUREN

Steve Van Buren was one of football's first great runners. He played in the NFL for eight seasons. Half of those seasons, he led the league in rushing yards and rushing touchdowns. Van Buren was the first player to rush for more than 1,000 yards more than once. He was also the first player to rush for more than 10 touchdowns in a season. He first accomplished that in 1945, when he scored 15 touchdowns. His 1945 season was one of the best individual seasons in NFL history. He led the league in three different categories: rushing yards, scoring, and kickoff return average.

Van Buren's first 1,000-yard rushing season was the first time the Philadelphia Eagles made the postseason. He rushed for 1,008 yards and 13 touchdowns in 1947. He led the league in both categories. He led in them the following two seasons as well. Those seasons resulted in NFL championships for the Eagles. Van Buren rushed for a career-high 1,146 yards in 1949. The 1949 NFL Championship Game was played in muddy conditions in Los Angeles. Van Buren drove through the slop, gaining 196 yards in the team's 14–0 win.

A year earlier, Van Buren nearly missed the 1948 NFL Championship Game in Philadelphia. A blizzard raged that day. Van Buren was sure the game was going to be postponed. It wasn't. His head coach frantically called him and got him to the game. Van Buren rushed for 98 yards and scored the game's only touchdown in the 7–0 win.

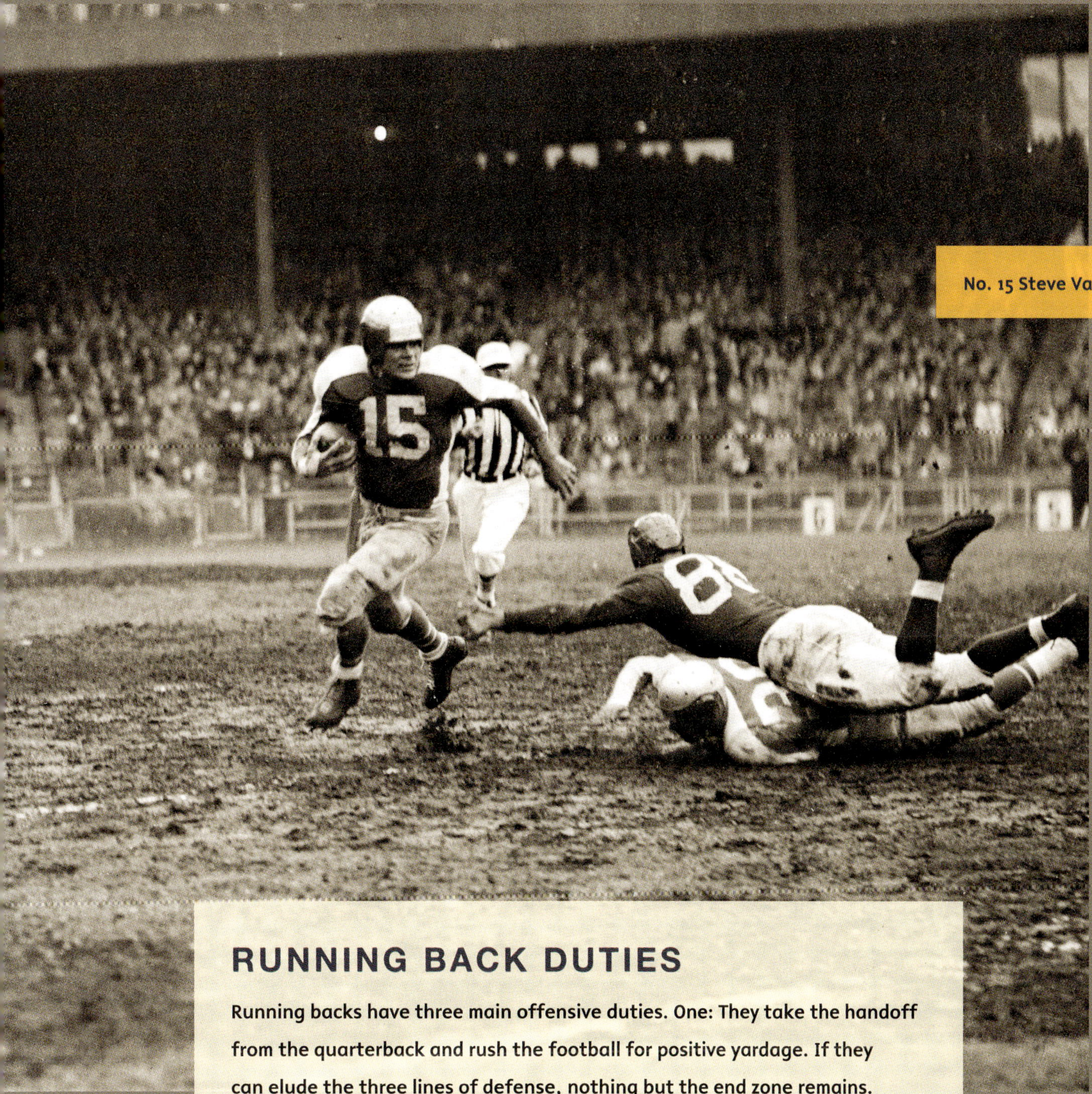
No. 15 Steve Van Buren

RUNNING BACK DUTIES

Running backs have three main offensive duties. One: They take the handoff from the quarterback and rush the football for positive yardage. If they can elude the three lines of defense, nothing but the end zone remains. Two: If running backs don't rush the ball, they act as reliable receivers. They are usually the safety net for the quarterback if the receivers downfield are covered. Three: Running backs may stay in the backfield and block the onrushing defender trying to get to the quarterback.

32

JIM BROWN

JIM BROWN (1936–2023)
FULLBACK
CLEVELAND BROWNS SEASONS: 1957–65
HALL OF FAME CLASS: 1971
AWARDS/HONORS: MEMBER OF NFL 75TH/100TH ANNIVERSARY TEAMS, 9X PRO BOWL, 9X ALL-PRO (8X FIRST TEAM), 1960S NFL ALL-DECADE TEAM, 3X NFL MOST VALUABLE PLAYER, NFL ROOKIE OF THE YEAR, NFL CHAMPION

One of the strongest rushers of his generation was Jim Brown. He played nine years in the NFL. He led the league in rushing yards eight times. Five times he led in rushing touchdowns. He retired after the 1965 season with an NFL record 12,312 rushing yards. That record stood until 1984.

Brown's greatness appeared in his very first season. He rushed for 942 yards and 9 touchdowns to lead the league in both categories. He was named NFL Most Valuable Player (MVP) and Rookie of the Year. Brown is the only player in history to achieve both awards in the same season. He only got better from there. He was named NFL MVP again the following season after rushing for 1,527 yards and 17 touchdowns. Brown rushed for 1,446 yards in 1964 to lead the Cleveland Browns to an NFL championship. Brown won MVP honors again in his final season of 1965. He averaged more than 104 rushing yards a game over his career. He is the only running back to average more than 100 yards a game in his career.

Brown shocked the league when he retired from football at just 30 years old. He pursued acting. He starred in several films after his football retirement. Fans still wonder how many more yards and honors Brown would have gained if he had played football longer.

O. J. SIMPSON

O. J. SIMPSON (1947–2024)
RUNNING BACK
BUFFALO BILLS SEASONS: 1969–77; SAN FRANCISCO 49ERS SEASONS: 1978–79
HALL OF FAME CLASS: 1985
AWARDS/HONORS: MEMBER OF NFL 75TH/100TH ANNIVERSARY TEAMS, 6X PRO BOWL, 5X FIRST TEAM ALL-PRO, 1970S NFL ALL-DECADE TEAM, NFL MOST VALUABLE PLAYER, NFL OFFENSIVE PLAYER OF THE YEAR

Orenthal James (O. J.) Simpson was already famous before he played in the NFL. Nicknamed "The Juice," Simpson had run for more than 1,700 yards and 22 touchdowns in his final season at the University of Southern California. He had also won the Heisman Trophy. The award goes to the best college football player of the season. As the number one overall pick in the 1969 common draft, Simpson was the easy choice for the Buffalo Bills.

The Bills were not a good team. They won just eight games over Simpson's first three years. Simpson had his first 1,000-yard season in 1972. His 1,251 yards led the league. The following season, Simpson became the first player to rush for more than 2,000 yards in a season. He rushed for 2,003 yards. He averaged 143.1 yards a game. That remains the highest mark in league history. He was named NFL MVP. Buffalo had their first winning record with Simpson. They reached the playoffs in 1974. Simpson rushed for 1,125 yards.

Simpson continued to rule the next two seasons. He rushed for more than 1,800 yards in 1975 and more than 1,500 yards in 1976. That capped a stretch of leading the league in rushing yards four of five seasons. Twice during that time, he led the league in rushing touchdowns, including 16 in 1975.

Simpson ran for more than 11,200 yards in his career. He had 61 rushing touchdowns, too. He made six Pro Bowls and was named a First Team All-Pro selection five times.

FRANCO HARRIS

FRANCO HARRIS (1950–2022)
RUNNING BACK
PITTSBURGH STEELERS SEASONS: 1972–83; SEATTLE SEAHAWKS SEASON: 1984
HALL OF FAME CLASS: 1990
AWARDS/HONORS: 9X PRO BOWL, 3X ALL-PRO (1X FIRST TEAM), 1970S NFL ALL-DECADE TEAM, NFL MAN OF THE YEAR, NFL OFFENSIVE ROOKIE OF THE YEAR, 4X SUPER BOWL CHAMPION, SUPER BOWL MVP

Franco Harris was a fantastic running back. But it was for one reception that he is best known. He made the "Immaculate Reception" for the Pittsburgh Steelers in 1972. It happened in an American Football Conference (AFC) Divisional Playoff game between the Steelers and the Oakland Raiders. Late in the game, a pass downfield was deflected. Harris caught the ball just before it hit the ground. He raced down the left sideline for the game-winning touchdown. The moment was part of a great rookie season for Harris. He rushed for 1,055 yards and 10 touchdowns. He was named NFL Offensive Rookie of the Year. That season was the first of his nine straight Pro Bowl seasons.

Harris excelled in big games for Pittsburgh, especially Super Bowls. In Super Bowl IX (9), following the 1974 season, Harris rushed for 158 yards and a touchdown. He helped the team win 16–6 over the Minnesota Vikings. He was named Super Bowl MVP. Three more Super Bowl titles were claimed by Harris and the Steelers in the 1970s. Harris rushed for a touchdown in Super Bowl XIII (13), following the 1978 season, and two more in the team's Super Bowl XIV (14) win the next season. By the end of his career, he held numerous postseason and Super Bowl records.

Harris retired with 12,120 career rushing yards and 91 rushing touchdowns. When he left the game, both stats ranked third all-time in NFL history. Harris rushed for more than 1,000 yards eight times.

32

Earl Campbell

UNBREAKABLE RECORD

The length of an NFL football field is 100 yards. That means the longest rushing play possible is 99 yards. Only two players have ever done it. The first was Hall of Famer Tony Dorsett of the Dallas Cowboys in the 1982 season. Playing against the Minnesota Vikings, Dorsett rushed through a big hole at the line. He outraced all defenders down the right sideline for a 99-yard touchdown run. Derrick Henry of the Tennessee Titans made the play in 2018. Henry broke through the Jacksonville Jaguars' defensive line and sprinted down the left sideline. He stiff-armed three defenders along the way to his own 99-yard touchdown run.

EARL CAMPBELL (1950–)
RUNNING BACK
HOUSTON OILERS SEASONS: 1978–84; NEW ORLEANS SAINTS SEASONS: 1984–85
HALL OF FAME CLASS: 1991
AWARDS/HONORS: MEMBER OF NFL 100TH ANNIVERSARY TEAM, 5X PRO BOWL, 3X FIRST TEAM ALL-PRO, 1970S NFL ALL-DECADE TEAM, NFL MOST VALUABLE PLAYER, 3X NFL OFFENSIVE PLAYER OF THE YEAR, NFL OFFENSIVE ROOKIE OF THE YEAR

EARL CAMPBELL

Earl Campbell had one of the greatest starts to an NFL career in history. He was already a force when he came into the league. He had won the Heisman Trophy in 1977 while playing for the University of Texas. He was taken number one overall in the 1978 NFL Draft by his home-state Houston Oilers. In his rookie season, Campbell rushed for a league-high 1,450 yards. He was named NFL Offensive Rookie of the Year and NFL Offensive Player of the Year (OPOY). He helped Houston reach the playoffs for the first time in nine years. Campbell did even better in 1979. He rushed for 1,697 yards and 19 touchdowns. Those stats led the NFL in both categories. Campbell earned OPOY again and was named NFL MVP. The Oilers reached the AFC Championship Game both seasons. But they lost to the Pittsburgh Steelers each time.

Despite the great honors of 1978 and 1979, Campbell's best season may have been 1980. He nearly became the second player to rush for 2,000 yards in a season. His season total of 1,934 yards and 13 rushing touchdowns led the league. Four times he rushed for at least 200 yards in a game that season—an NFL record. He was named OPOY for the third straight season. He was also runner-up in NFL MVP voting.

Campbell rushed for more than 1,300 yards two more times before retiring. He finished his eight-year career with 9,407 rushing yards and 74 rushing touchdowns.

WALTER PAYTON

WALTER PAYTON (1953–99)
RUNNING BACK
CHICAGO BEARS SEASONS: 1975–87
HALL OF FAME CLASS: 1993
AWARDS/HONORS: MEMBER OF NFL 75TH/100TH ANNIVERSARY TEAMS, 9X PRO BOWL, 8X ALL-PRO (5X FIRST TEAM), 1970S/1980S NFL ALL-DECADE TEAMS, NFL MOST VALUABLE PLAYER, NFL MAN OF THE YEAR, NFL OFFENSIVE PLAYER OF THE YEAR, SUPER BOWL CHAMPION

He was the man they called "Sweetness." It was a nickname running back Walter Payton got while playing at Jackson State University. He had the personality and athleticism that drew people to him. He also had the ability to play through any problems. He missed only one non-strike game over his 13-year football career with the Chicago Bears. In a 1977 game against the Minnesota Vikings, Payton rushed for a then-single-game NFL record of 275 yards. He did that while suffering from the flu. In 1984, Payton broke the career rushing yards record once held by Jim Brown. He finished with a career rushing total of 16,726 yards. That record stood until Emmitt Smith broke it in 2002. Payton's mark still ranks second all-time.

Payton's best season was 1977. He led the league in rushing yards with 1,852 and in rushing touchdowns with 14. He was named the NFL Most Valuable Player and NFL Offensive Player of the Year. He helped the Bears reach the playoffs for the first time in 14 years. Payton reached at least 1,000 yards rushing in 10 seasons. He was selected to play in nine Pro Bowls and was named First Team All-Pro five times. He finally won a Super Bowl championship following the 1985 season.

Payton won the NFL's Man of the Year award in 1977. It recognizes achievements by a player for community service. The award was renamed in Payton's honor following his death in 1999. The NFL regards it as the league's highest honor.

ERIC DICKERSON

ERIC DICKERSON (1960–)
RUNNING BACK
LOS ANGELES RAMS SEASONS: 1983–87; INDIANAPOLIS COLTS SEASONS: 1987–91; LOS ANGELES RAIDERS SEASON: 1992; ATLANTA FALCONS SEASON: 1993
HALL OF FAME CLASS: 1999
AWARDS/HONORS: MEMBER OF NFL 100TH ANNIVERSARY TEAM, 6X PRO BOWL, 5X FIRST TEAM ALL-PRO, 1980S NFL ALL-DECADE TEAM, NFL OFFENSIVE PLAYER OF THE YEAR, NFL OFFENSIVE ROOKIE OF THE YEAR

Eric Dickerson started setting records the moment he first stepped foot on an NFL field. In his 1983 NFL rookie season, he set rookie records for rushing attempts (390), rushing yards (1,808), and rushing touchdowns (18). The 1,808 rushing yards led the league in 1983. The next season was even better. Dickerson set the single-season rushing record with 2,105 yards. That total shattered O. J. Simpson's record of 2,003. Dickerson's record stood as of 2024.

Dickerson continued to put up big numbers. In 1985, he set the single-game postseason rushing record with 248 yards. It happened in an NFC Divisional Playoff win over the Dallas Cowboys. In 1986, Dickerson led the league again in rushing with 1,821 yards. He was named NFL Offensive Player of the Year. He led the Los Angeles Rams to the playoffs in each of his first four seasons. Although he was traded to the Indianapolis Colts early in the 1987 season, Dickerson did not stop running. He rushed for more than 1,000 yards in just nine games with the Colts. In his first full season with the Colts, in 1988, he led the league again with 1,659 yards. He also collected 14 rushing touchdowns.

Dickerson rushed for 13,259 career yards. He retired in 1993 as the second all-time leading rusher in NFL history. He was selected for six Pro Bowls and was a five-time First Team All-Pro selection.

BARRY SANDERS

BARRY SANDERS (1968–)
RUNNING BACK
DETROIT LIONS SEASONS: 1989–98
HALL OF FAME CLASS: 2004
AWARDS/HONORS: MEMBER OF NFL 100TH ANNIVERSARY TEAM, 10X PRO BOWL, 10X ALL-PRO (6X FIRST TEAM), 1990S NFL ALL-DECADE TEAM, NFL MOST VALUABLE PLAYER, 2X NFL OFFENSIVE PLAYER OF THE YEAR, NFL OFFENSIVE ROOKIE OF THE YEAR

Barry Sanders came into the NFL with a lot of hype. In 1988, he put together one of the greatest seasons in college football history. He set single-season records for rushing yards (2,628) and rushing touchdowns (37) that stood as of 2024. The Detroit Lions selected him with the third overall pick of the 1989 NFL Draft. Sanders went on to play 10 seasons in the NFL, all with the Lions. Each season, he was selected for the Pro Bowl. And each season, he was named either a First Team or Second Team All-Pro selection.

Sanders had a fantastic rookie season in 1989, rushing for 1,470 yards and 14 touchdowns. That season was the first of his 10 straight 1,000-yard rushing seasons. Sanders was the first to record a streak like that. The following season, he led the league in rushing yards for the first time. He did so three more times. His greatest season was 1997. But it didn't start well. Sanders gained just 53 yards over the first two games. Over the last 14 games, though, he ran for 2,000. Sanders became just the third player to rush for 2,000 yards in a season. He was named NFL MVP. Sanders led the league in rushing four times (1990, 1994, 1996, 1997).

Sanders retired unexpectedly following the 1998 season. He was 31 years old. He had collected 15,269 career rushing yards. That mark ranks fourth all-time.

EMMITT SMITH

EMMITT SMITH (1969–)
RUNNING BACK
DALLAS COWBOYS SEASONS: 1990–2002; ARIZONA CARDINALS SEASONS: 2003–04
HALL OF FAME CLASS: 2010
AWARDS/HONORS: MEMBER OF NFL 100TH ANNIVERSARY TEAM, 8X PRO BOWL, 5X ALL-PRO (4X FIRST TEAM), 1990S NFL ALL-DECADE TEAM, NFL MOST VALUABLE PLAYER, NFL OFFENSIVE ROOKIE OF THE YEAR, 3X SUPER BOWL CHAMPION, SUPER BOWL MVP, NFL CAREER RUSHING LEADER

Emmitt Smith was a workhorse. He didn't miss many games over his 15-year Hall of Fame career. He led the league in rushing attempts three times. Quite simply, Smith was good at what he did. He was so good that he topped Walter Payton's career mark in 2002. Smith ended his career as the NFL all-time career rushing leader. He retired with 18,355 career rushing yards. He also tops the list in career rushing touchdowns with 164.

Smith earned NFL Offensive Rookie of the Year in 1990 with 937 rushing yards. He did even better in 1991. His 1,563 rushing yards led the league. It was the first of 11 straight 1,000-yard rushing seasons. Smith again led the league in 1992 with 1,713 yards and 18 touchdowns. He helped lead the Dallas Cowboys to a Super Bowl win. Smith missed the first two games the following season over a contract dispute. The Cowboys lost both games and then quickly signed him to a new contract. Despite missing those two games, Smith again led the NFL in rushing yards with 1,486. He was named NFL MVP. He led Dallas to another Super Bowl title. In the 30–13 win over the Buffalo Bills, Smith rushed for 132 yards and 2 touchdowns. He was named Super Bowl MVP.

Smith led the league in rushing for a fourth time in 1995. He set a then-single-season NFL record with 25 rushing touchdowns. With Smith, the Cowboys won their third Super Bowl in four years.

MARSHALL FAULK

MARSHALL FAULK (1973–)
RUNNING BACK
INDIANAPOLIS COLTS SEASONS: 1994–98; ST. LOUIS RAMS SEASONS: 1999–2005
HALL OF FAME CLASS: 2011
AWARDS/HONORS: 7X PRO BOWL, 6X ALL-PRO (3X FIRST TEAM), NFL MOST VALUABLE PLAYER, 3X NFL OFFENSIVE PLAYER OF THE YEAR, NFL OFFENSIVE ROOKIE OF THE YEAR, SUPER BOWL CHAMPION

Marshall Faulk was one of the most versatile running backs in NFL history. Not only could he rush the football, but he was also a reliable receiver. The Indianapolis Colts knew this when they selected him with the number two overall pick in the 1994 NFL Draft. In his first season, Faulk rushed for 1,282 yards. He also had 52 receptions for 522 yards. He was named NFL Offensive Rookie of the Year. He continued to put up big numbers. Even so, the Colts traded him after the 1998 season to the St. Louis Rams.

The Rams were a terrible team when Faulk arrived in 1999. Their last winning season had been 1989. But with Faulk, St. Louis turned itself around. Faulk rushed for 1,381 yards. He had career highs in receptions (87) and receiving yards (1,048). He became just the second player in NFL history to both rush and receive for 1,000 yards in a season. Faulk was named NFL Offensive Player of the Year (OPOY). The Rams went on to win the Super Bowl. Faulk scored 26 total touchdowns in 2000. He was named both NFL MVP and NFL OPOY. He won his third straight NFL OPOY award in 2001. The Rams returned to the Super Bowl following a 14-win season.

Faulk became the first player in NFL history to gain at least 2,000 yards from scrimmage in four straight seasons. Scrimmage yards combine rushing and receiving yards. Faulk ranks sixth all-time with 19,154 career scrimmage yards.

28
54

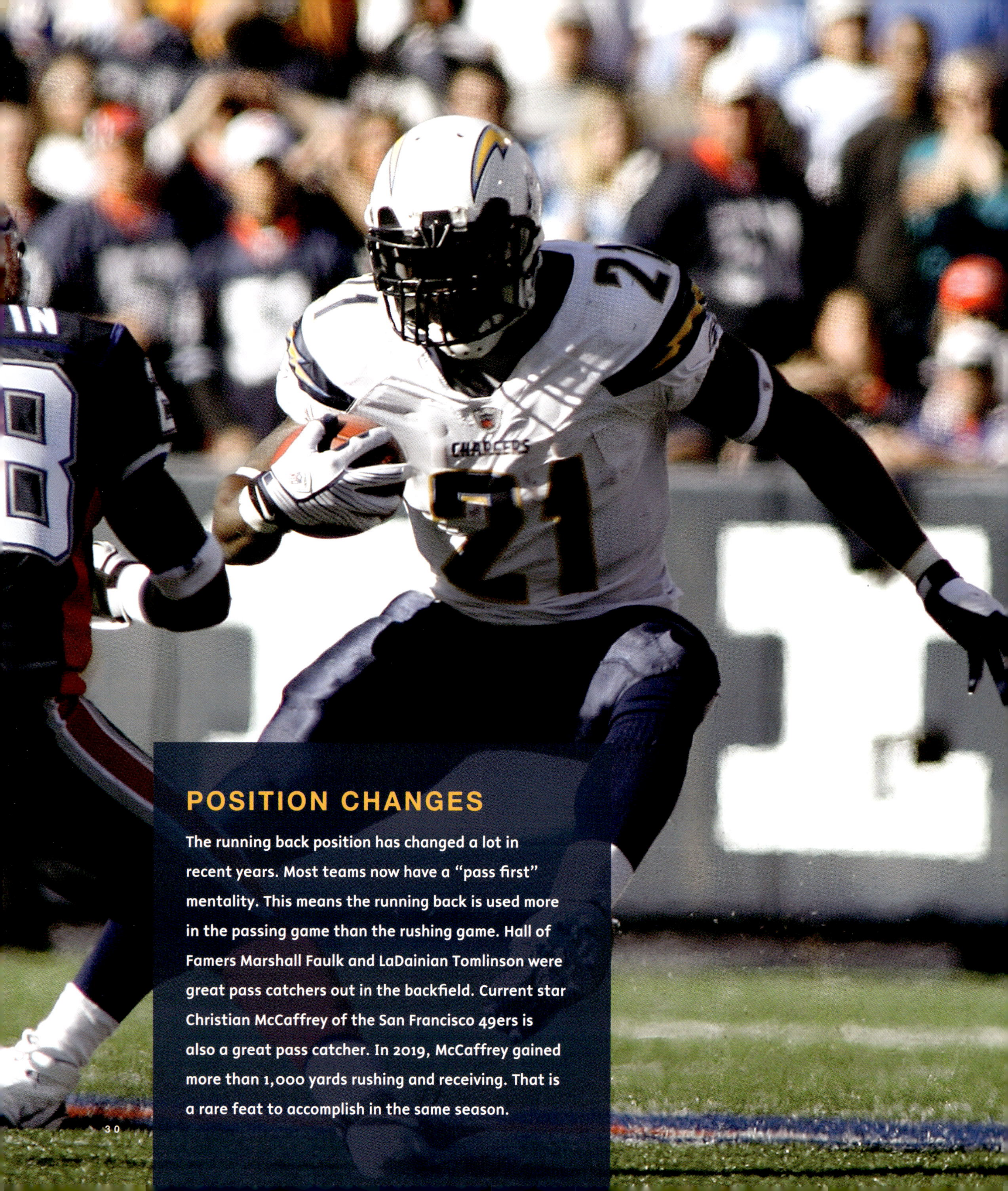

POSITION CHANGES

The running back position has changed a lot in recent years. Most teams now have a "pass first" mentality. This means the running back is used more in the passing game than the rushing game. Hall of Famers Marshall Faulk and LaDainian Tomlinson were great pass catchers out in the backfield. Current star Christian McCaffrey of the San Francisco 49ers is also a great pass catcher. In 2019, McCaffrey gained more than 1,000 yards rushing and receiving. That is a rare feat to accomplish in the same season.

LADAINIAN TOMLINSON

LADAINIAN TOMLINSON (1979–)
RUNNING BACK
SAN DIEGO CHARGERS SEASONS: 2001–09; NEW YORK JETS SEASONS: 2010–11
HALL OF FAME CLASS: 2017
AWARDS/HONORS: 5X PRO BOWL, 6X ALL-PRO (3X FIRST TEAM), 2000S NFL ALL-DECADE TEAM, NFL MOST VALUABLE PLAYER, NFL OFFENSIVE PLAYER OF THE YEAR, NFL MAN OF THE YEAR

LaDainian Tomlinson was already setting records prior to his NFL career. He was the first NCAA Division I player in history to rush for at least 400 yards in one game. He rushed for more than 2,000 yards his senior season at Texas Christian University. The San Diego Chargers selected him fifth overall in the 2001 NFL Draft. He continued to put up strong numbers in the pros. He rushed for 1,236 yards and 10 touchdowns in his rookie season. He was also a reliable receiver. In 2003, Tomlinson had 100 receptions. He is one of only five running backs in NFL history to catch at least 100 passes in a season.

What Tomlinson did best was run the football. He rushed for more than 1,100 yards in each of his first eight seasons. His best season was 2006. He set a single-season NFL record with 28 rushing touchdowns. He added three more receiving for 31 total touchdowns. Tomlinson rushed for 1,815 yards to lead the league and had 508 yards receiving. He was the easy choice for NFL Most Valuable Player. Tomlinson repeated as the league's leading rusher in 2007 with 1,474 yards and 15 touchdowns.

Tomlinson found the end zone often in his Hall of Fame career. His 145 career rushing touchdowns rank second all-time. His 162 total touchdowns are third all-time. He ranks seventh all-time in career rushing yards with 13,684.

INDEX